If Me Really Ruled the World

It's clean(ish)
and it's funny

Edited by
Vincent Furnier

West One
PUBLISHING

© West One Publishing Ltd, 1999
Edited by Vincent Furnier
Illustrations by Martin Impey

With special thanks to Nikki Esson

A CIP catalogue record for this book is available from the
British Library.
ISBN 1 900327 53 8

Published by
West One (Trade) Publishing Ltd
Kestrel House
Dukes Place
Marlow
Bucks SL7 2QH

Telephone: 01628 487722
Fax: 01628 487724
E-mail: sales@west-one.com

To Michael Shelton,

who knows a thing or two

about laughing.

With particular thanks to
Damian Harrison, Jamie Fleming, Charles Maynard,
Dave Headon, Jane Bramwell, Sarrena Hall,
Kate Hindle and Linda Harrow.

"Sweet is revenge –
especially for women."

Lord Bryon

If men really ruled the World...

Any fake 'phone number that a girl gave you would automatically forward your call to her real number.

Nodding and looking at your watch would be deemed an acceptable response to: "I love you."

Hallmark cards would make 'Sorry, what's your name again?' cards.

When your girlfriend/wife/partner needs to talk to you during the match, she'll appear in a little box in a corner of the TV screen during half time.

Birth control would come in lager, bitter or stout.

If Men Ruled the World...

The funniest guy in the office
would get to be chief executive.

"Sorry I'm late, but I got really wasted
last night," would be an acceptable excuse
for tardiness at the office.

It would be considered harmless fun
to gather 30 friends, put on horned helmets
and go pillage towns in Essex.

Lifeguards could remove citizens
from beaches for violating
the 'public ugliness' by-laws.

Remember...

Everything comes to he who goes
after what the other guy is waiting for.

We'd learn that power corrupts, but
absolute power is even more fun.

We'd make sure that women should
be obscene and not heard.

Instead of a beer belly,
you'd get 'beer biceps'.

St Patrick's Day would remain the same,
but it would be celebrated every month.

If Men Ruled the World...

Instead of an expensive engagement ring, you could present your wife-to-be with a giant foam hand that said: "You're No. 1."

St Valentine's Day would be moved to 29th February, so that all that hearts and flowers nonsense happened only every four years.

The only TV programme opposite Match of the Day would be European Football from a different camera angle.

"Some men try to climb mountains, others try to date them."

Anon

Every man would get four real
'Get out of Jail Free' cards every year.

Taps would run 'Hot', 'Cold'
and '100% Proof'.

If Men Ruled the World...

Telephones would cut off automatically after 30 seconds of conversation.

Whether you're married or single, you could just leave your dirty clothes for the Laundry Fairy to take away, launder and return to your cupboard.

Avoid banishment to the spare room – fill the spare room with exercise equipment or football fanzines, so that the bed is completely unapproachable even when you are completely plastered.

When a copper gave you a ticket, every smart-Alec answer you gave would actually reduce your ticket, for example:

Policeman:
Do you know how fast you were going?
You:
All I know is, I was spilling my beer all over the place.
Policeman:
Nice one – that's £10 off.

If at first you did succeed, try not to look astonished.

Reality is an illusion caused by a lack of alcohol.

The Ten Answers
Men used to be afraid to give
to women's stupid questions
(but not any more!)...

1. No, we can't be friends;
I just want to use you for sex.

2. Ha! You've got a fat chance of me calling you.

3. The rubbish can take itself out.

4. Well, yes, actually I do this all the time.

5. I hate your bloody friends.

6. Your mother is a terrible old bag.

7. I have every intention of using you, and no
intention of speaking to you again after tonight.

8. I'd rather watch football.

9. I'd prefer to stick hot needles in my
eyeballs than do that.

10. No, the dress doesn't make you look fat. It's all the ice cream, chocolate and biscuits you eat that make you look fat.

Remember...

"Give a woman an inch
and she thinks, she's a ruler."

Anon

"Why haven't women
got labels on their foreheads saying:
'Danger; Government Health Warning:
women can seriously damage your brains,
genitals, current account, confidence,
razor blades and good standing among
your friends'?"

Jeffrey Barnard, 'The Spectator'

"Dally not with money or women."

17th Century Proverb

Man to man...

My wife and I have the secret of making a marriage last. Twice a week we go to a little restaurant, have a little wine, good food... she goes Tuesdays, and I go Fridays.

"Praise makes good men better and bad men worse."

18th Century Proverb

"Boys will be boys."

17th Century Proverb

"Deeds are male and words are female."

16th Century Proverb

30 rules for being a proper man...

1. **Don't call,** ever.

2. If you **don't like** a girl, **don't** tell her. It's more fun to let her **work it out** by herself.

3. **Lie.** Deny everything.

4. Be as **ambiguous** as possible. If you **don't feel** like answering, a nice **grunt will do.**

5. Don't forget: **you're a man, so it isn't** your fault.

6. Girls find it attractive if a man has had more women than baths.

7. Women like it when you ignore them. It arouses them.

8. Vanity is a most important trait for a man. Check your hair, clothing, good looks, etc. every time you pass a reflective surface.

9. Don't wear matching clothes. People will think your girlfriend or partner picked them out – which will cramp your style when picking up girls.

10. Every sentence that anyone says can be contorted to have a sexual meaning.

11. Practise your blank stare.

12. Feelings? What feelings?

13. 'Love' is not in your vocabulary,
except in the phrases: "I'd love a beer," or,
"I'd love to go to the footie."

14. A general rule: if whatever you're doing
doesn't satisfy you completely in five minutes,
it's not really worth it.

15. Dump your girlfriend.
Beg and plead 'til you get her back.
Dump her again. Repeat.

16. Always apologise. Never mean it.

17. Don't ever notice anything.

18. General rule: different is BAD.

19. Try to have a good memory. But it is OK to forget trivia such as your girl's birthday and her eye colour.

20. If people express extreme disgust at whatever you're doing – don't stop. This is the desired reaction!

21. Females don't care what you do to them as long as they get to please you.

22. Basic fundamental rule of dating: quantity not quality.

23. Basic fundamental rule of sex: quantity is quality.

24. You are male, therefore you are superior.

25. If you **cheat** on a girl, but **no-one** finds out, **technically** you've done nothing **wrong**.

26. If the **question** begins: "Why…" **the answer** is: "I don't know."

27. Keep track of how **many** seconds in **your** life you have **thought** about sex. **Compare** with others.

28. If you are ever forced to **show emotion**, just pick **random** emotions like rage, lust or insanity and display them at **random,** inconvenient times. You **won't** be asked to do it again.

29. Beer, **more beer,** and for **afters** – beer.

30. **One** word: Football.

Choosing the man at the top...

You have to elect a world leader, and
your vote counts, so consider the profiles of these
candidates to see which would get your vote:

Candidate A   Consults with astrologers
Has two mistresses
Chain-smokes and drinks
8-10 martinis a day
Is in general poor health

Candidate B   Kicked out of office twice
Sleeps until noon
Used opium in college
Drinks 2 pints of brandy every evening

Candidate C   Decorated war hero
Vegetarian
Doesn't smoke
Drinks the occasional beer
Hasn't had any illicit love affairs

Which would you choose?

A = Roosevelt   B = Churchill   C = Hitler

10 things men should know about women...

You'll never understand them, so stop trying.

They will drive you crazy/to drink/to an early grave.

When they say they won't be a minute,
they're always right.

Sorry, crying is part of the deal.

They will spend your life's savings
getting great bargains.

You will always know where you are – in the wrong.

Chocolates and/or flowers can get you
out of life-threatening situations.

Whatever it is, you will never have done enough.

There isn't a laundry fairy that miraculously
picks and cleans your clothes. It's her.

Like it or not, you can't do without them –
but a 6-pack and a pizza is a good second.

Warning for men:

It takes many nails to build a crib, but only one screw to fill it.

"Is there life after marriage?"
Graffiti

Marriages, friends and other relationships...

Wife:
Let's go out and have some fun tonight!
Husband:
OK, but if you get home before I do, leave the hall light on, will you?

Losing a wife can be difficult.
In my case, it was almost impossible.

Some men are brave.
Others are bachelors.

The worst an honest man can do is make an honest mistake.

Remember...

Never go to bed furious.
Stay up and fight.

Contraception is just avoiding the issue.

Seduction is the art
of genital persuasion.

I haven't spoken to my wife for 18 months –
I don't like to interrupt her.

Man to woman:

I could explain it to you,
but your brain would explode.

Questions and Answers...

Q What's the most common cause of
hearing loss amongst men?
A The wife says she wants
to talk to him.

Q Why is a bachelor skinny and
a married man fat?
A The single man takes one look
in the 'fridge and goes to bed.
The married man takes one look in
the bed and goes to the 'fridge.

Q Why is a woman like a condom?
A It spends more time in your wallet.

Remember...

The world beats a path to your door only when you're in the bathroom.

Man to man:

I've been in love with the same woman for years. If my wife ever finds out, she'll kill me!

Questions and Answers…

Q What are the three words
you dread most when making love?
A Darling, I'm home.

Q What's the difference between
a Catholic wife and a Jewish wife?
A A Catholic wife has real
orgasms and fake jewellery.

Q Why did God create man first?
A He didn't want
a woman looking over his
shoulder criticising.

Q What do you call a woman who's lost 95% of her intelligence? A Divorced.

Q How do men define a 50-50 relationship? A She cooks, I eat. She cleans, I dirty. She irons, I wrinkle.

Q What do you tell a woman with two black eyes? A Nothing; she's been told – twice.

Q Why do most men die before their wives? A Because they want to.

Advice for men:

Never do card tricks for the group you play poker with.

Questions and Answers...

Q What is the one thing that all men in singles bars have in common?
A They're all married.

Q What's the difference between a girlfriend and a wife?
A About 3 stone.

Q What's the difference between a terrorist and a mother-in-law?
A You can negotiate with a terrorist.

A dim woman...

It's Friday night and Joe and his wife
are sharing an intimate moment, but he gets
increasingly irritated when she isn't
showing any signs of enjoyment at all.

"Why don't you moan when we make love?"
he asks crossly.

So matters progress, she sighs,
and then starts up with:
"Why don't you mow the lawn?
You never take the rubbish out.
Why are you so mean to my mother?.."

Warning for men...

If you want to trigger World War III,
just mention that old favourite,
the biological clock, to a girl in her 30s.

Sorry:

The secret of a happy marriage remains a secret.

A question:

Do infants enjoy infancy as much
as adults enjoy adultery?

Q Why do men like love at first sight?
A Because they know it's all over as
soon as she opens her mouth.

Q What's a man's idea of a sophisticated cocktail?

A A pint of beer with an olive in it.

Oh brother...

Graham's wife was sick of her husband's

heavy drinking.

One night she decided to give him a fright.

She made herself up to look like the devil

and went down to the local cemetery.

She knew that her husband always took

a short cut through the cemetery on his

way home from the pub.

It was not long before he came staggering

along between the tombstones.

She leapt out shouting:

"Ha ha ha! Do you know who I am?"

He jumped back at first, startled.

Then he relaxed and smiled and said,

"'Course I do."

"I'm the Devil – aren't you afraid of me?"

"Nope."

"Why not?"

"Why should I be? I've been married to your sister for years."

A bit of a poser?

If your wife and a lawyer were drowning,
and you had to choose, would you
go to lunch or to a movie?

John:
Do you know,
I haven't had sex in two years!

Martin:
Celibate, eh?

John:
No, married

Q What do you call a basement full of women?
A A whine cellar.

After death do you part...

A group of men are standing outside the pearly gates, waiting to get into Heaven.

St. Peter approaches and declares:
"All you men who were henpecked by your wives during your lives, go to the left wall. All those who weren't, go to the right wall."

All the men go to the left wall except one timid little old man who goes to the right wall.

St. Peter eyes him.
"Just a moment, all those who were henpecked were asked to go the left wall.
So why have you gone to the right wall?"

"My wife told me to."

It doesn't always pay
to advertise…

A man inserted an advertisement
in the local paper classifieds.
'Wife wanted.'
The next day he received hundreds
of letters. They all said the same thing:
'Have mine.'

When a man has married a wife,
he finds out whether
Her knees and elbows are only
glued together.

Marriage, by William Blake

"Men are April when they woo,
December when they wed:
Maids are May when they are maids
But the sky changes when they are wives."

Shakespeare, As you like it.

"Advice to persons about to marry –
don't."

Punch, 1845

"Give a man a free hand, and
he'll run it all over you."

Mae West

"Woman are made to be loved,
not understood."

Oscar Wilde

10 points about marriage from the male perspective...

Just think, if it **weren't** for marriage, men would go through life thinking they had **no faults** at all.

In the **beginning,** God created **earth** and rested. Then **God created man** and rested. Then God **created** woman. **Since then,** neither **God** nor **man** has rested.

My wife and I **are inseparable.** In fact, last week **it took four** police officers and a dog.

Do **you know** the punishment for bigamy? **Two mothers-in-law.**

Most men **define marriage** as an expensive way to get **your laundry** done.

The last fight we had was my fault.
She asked, "What's on the TV?"
I said, 'Dust.'

If you want your wife to listen and pay undivided
attention to every word you say, talk in your sleep.

There was a man who said,
"I never knew what real happiness was until
I got married, and then it was too late."

A little boy asked his father:
"How much does it cost to get married?"
His father replied:
"I don't know, son; I'm still paying for it."

All marriages should come with a health warning –
it's one thing loving a wife, but getting her family
as part of the deal is enough to drive you to drink.

"Choose your wife rather by your ear than your eye."

18th Century Proverb

"The only really happy people are married women and single men."

H.L. Mencken, American Journalist 1880 – 1956

"Wedlock is padlock."

Proverb 1678

"A bachelor lives like a king and dies like a beggar."

Attributed to L.S. Lowry

"Women are like elephants to me; they're nice to look at but I wouldn't want to own one."

W.C. Fields

"Man is as old as he feels, and a woman as old as she looks."

20th Century Proverb

"A drunken **night** makes a **cloudy** morning."
18th Century Proverb

"**Women** are **necessary** evils."
16th Century Proverb

"Brigands **demand** your money or your life;
women **require** both."

Reminder for men...

Marriage is more than just a word;
it's a sentence.

"Marriage is like a cage:
one sees the birds outside desperate to get in,
and those inside equally desperate to get out."

Michel de Montaigne

"A sort of friendship recognised by the police."

R.L. Stevenson on matrimony

I would be married, but I'd have no wife.
I would be married to a single life.

The perfect marriage, by Richard Crashaw

One wife is too much for one husband to hear,
But two at a time there's no mortal can bear.

Not so gay, by John Gay

Epitaph on a tombstone:

Oops...

A man was complaining to his friend over several beers.

"I had it all – money, a beautiful house, a big car, the love of a beautiful woman, and suddenly: POW! It's all gone!"

"What happened?" asked his friend.

"My wife found out."

I will marry the next woman who says any or all of the following:

Are you sure you've had enough to drink?

Shouldn't you be down the pub with your mates?

I've decided to stop wearing clothes around the house.

You're so sexy when you're hung-over.

I'd rather watch football and drink beer with you than go shopping.

Hey – let's go down the shops so you can gorp at the girls' bums.

I love it when you play golf on Saturdays – I just wish you had time to play on Sundays, too.

Darling, our new neighbour's daughter is sunbathing again – do come and see.

Your mother is 'way better than mine.

Do me a favour, forget the stupid Valentine's Day thing – buy yourself some new golf clubs instead.

The 5 questions that men fear women askings...

The following questions are guaranteed to spark a major argument if the man answers truthfully. Therefore avoid the explosion by reading this analysis:

1. What are you thinking about?

Proper answer:

"I'm a bit pensive, I'm sorry, dear. I was just thinking what a wonderful warm human being you are and how lucky I am."

Truthful answer:

It could be any of the following:

That goal that decided the game.
I fancy going for a kip.

How fat you are.

Beer.

How much prettier she is than you.

How I would spend the insurance money if you died.

Nothing in particular, brain in neutral.

2. Do you love me?

Proper answer:

"Yes!" which must be said without hesitation.
Alternatively, for a more detail response, say:
"Yes, dear."

Truthful answer:

Oh yeah.

Would you feel better if I lied and said yes?

It depends on your definition of love.

Does it matter?
Who – me?

3. Do I look fat?

Proper answer:
"Of course not!"

Truthful answer:

Compared to...?

Well, you're not fat, but I wouldn't call you thin either.

That little bit of extra weight looks good on you.

I've seen fatter.

Sorry – say that again? I was just wondering how I would spend the insurance money if you died.

4. Do you think she's prettier than me?

Proper answer:

"Of course not!" – note emphatic tone.

Truthful answer:

Ah, but you have a better personality.

Not prettier, but thinner – definitely thinner.

Not as pretty as you were at the same age.

Define pretty for me.

Sorry – say that again? I was just wondering how I would spend the insurance money if you died.

5. What would you do if I died?

Don't even try to answer this – especially with the truthful answer that probably includes the purchase of a sports car and a speedboat with the insurance money.

A rhyme inscribed on a pint pot...

There are several reasons for drinking
And one has just entered my head;
If a man cannot drink when he's living
How the hell can he drink when he's dead?

Anon

Male singlemindedness...

A man walked into a bar and
ordered a glass of orange.
After a moment, the barman asked, "Still?"

The man replied: "Yes, I'm not a woman.
I haven't changed my bloody mind!"

Something for the weekend...

Standing at a check out, a teenage boy spots a display of condoms.

"Hey, Dad, what's a three pack for?" asks the spotty pubescent.

"For the weekend – two for Friday, one for Saturday."

"Then, Dad, what's a six pack for?"

"That's for when she moves into your pad – two for Friday night, two for Saturday and two for Sunday."

"Then, Dad, what's a twelve pack for?"

"That's for when you're married – one for January, one for February, one for March..."

Silly me...

After a quarrel, Lucy said to her husband:
"You know, I was a fool when I married you."

Her husband replied:
"Yes, dear, but I was in love and didn't notice."

"An alcoholic is someone you don't like
who drinks as much as you do."
Attributed to Dylan Thomas

"Most women are not so young as they are painted."
Max Beerbohm

"My wife dresses to kill. She cooks the same way."
Henry Youngman

Man to man...

Gerry: My wife's an angel!
Brian: You're lucky – mine's still alive.

Warning to men...

Don't **even** try to follow
a woman's line of **thinking**.
It's **heavily** mined.

Women like silent men.
They think **they're** listening.

The older **you** get, the **better**
you **realise** you were.

I doubt, **therefore** I might be.

Give a man **a fish** and **he'll eat** for a day.
Teach him **how to fish** and he'll sit in a boat
all day, **drink beer** and **eat 'til** he's taken up
the slack **on his waistband.**

If you can't be right, be loud.

Let her know the romance is over gently – get her name removed from your tattoo.

Women dream of world peace, a safe environment and eliminating hunger. Men dream of being stuck in a lift with Pamela Anderson and Melissa Messenger.

Women would come to learn that, when a man is behind the wheel of his car, he is not only all powerful, he is always, always right.

Did you hear about the man who finally worked women out? He died laughing before he could tell anyone.

Warning for men...

If your woman hands you the car keys and says:
"No, you drive. You drive so beautifully,
so confidently..." etc., be suspicious.
It probably means she thinks it's her turn
to have a few drinks.

Man to man...

"Can you beat my total of 63 women?"
"Only if you supply the whips."

She ran after the rubbish van shouting,
"Am I too late for the rubbish?"
"No," I cried, "Jump in."

Warning for women...

It begins when you sink into his arms;
it ends with your arms in his sink.

A big, swanky car cannot be a manhood substitute,
or surely men would be continually trying to park
in other people's garages and parking spaces.

Man to man...

"I take my wife everywhere,
but she keeps finding her way back."

When a man steals your wife, there is no
better revenge than to let him keep her.

Male logic...

"I've used up all my sick days so I'm calling in dead."

More male logic...

Men say stupid things because they like to – it's a joy to see a woman frustrated by a few simple, well-chosen words.

Physciatrist to man...

"Are you ever troubled by immoral thoughts?"
"No, Doctor, I really enjoy them."

Man to man...

Eric:

My first wife ate poisoned mushrooms.

Brian:

How terrible! And your second?

Eric:

She ate poisoned mushrooms.

Brian:

And your third ate poisoned mushrooms too?

Eric:

Oh no – she broke her neck.

Brian:

Oh, I see, an accident.

Eric:

Not exactly – she wouldn't eat her mushrooms.

Guidance for women...

Men have to ogle other women – it's a testosterone thing. Testosterone doesn't evaporate the moment he meets her. Women do it, too, and use some sort of photographic memory thing to store every detail for later reference. Men lack this ability, so they have to burn it into their memory by staring, which means they always get caught ogling.

Dirty message...

Napoleon to Josephine:
Don't wash.
I'm coming home.

Physical explanations...

We men can sit on our arses all day without moving because we have powerful sitting muscles. These have evolved since prehistoric times when we learnt to sit for extended periods while hunting prey. The more successful hunter was the one who could wait the longest – and therefore lived to pass this skill on to future generations.

Men hate shopping because...

We're used to hunting while the women gather. We prefer to go out, kill it and bring it back. We don't want to spend hours looking at things we have no intention of killing.

A guide to understanding
what a woman means...

What she says	What she means
Yes.	No.
No.	Yes.
Maybe.	No.
I'm sorry.	You'll be sorry.
We need...	I want...
It's your decision.	The correct decision is obvious, isn't it?
Do what you want.	You'll pay for this later.
We need to talk.	I want to complain.
OK, go ahead.	I don't want you to.
I'm not upset.	Of course I'm bloody upset!

You're very attentive.	Is sex the only thing you think about?
Be romantic, turn out the lights.	I have flabby thighs.
I want new curtains.	and carpet and furniture and a kitchen.
I heard a noise.	Oh, were you nearly asleep?
Do you love me?	I want something expensive.
How much do you love me?	I did something you won't like.
You have to learn to communicate.	Just agree with me.
I'm not shouting.	I'm shouting because it's important.
The same old thing.	Nothing.
Nothing.	Everything.
Everything.	PMT

A guide to understanding what a man means...

What he says	What he means
I'm hungry.	I'm hungry.
I'm sleepy.	I'm sleepy.
I'm tired.	I'm tired.
Do you want to go to a film?	I'd like to have sex with you.
Can I take you out to dinner?	I'd like to have sex with you.
Do you want to dance?	I'd like to have sex with you.
Nice dress!	Nice cleavage!
You look tense, let me give you a massage	Let me fondle you.

What's wrong?	What's the big deal?
What's wrong?	So sex is out of the question tonight then?
I'm bored.	I'd like to have sex with you.
I love you.	I'd like to have sex with you now.
I like the new haircut.	I liked the way it was before.
I like the new haircut.	£30 and it looks much the same.
Let's talk.	I'm trying to impress you by showing you that I'm a deep, meaningful person, and then maybe you'll have sex with me.
Will you marry me?	It'll stop you having sex with other men.
I like that dress better.	Can we go home now?

Men's advice for women...

1. Never buy a 'new' brand of beer because it was 'on sale'.

2. If we're in the garden and the TV is still on in the sitting room, it doesn't mean we're not watching it.

3. Wearing your new lingerie only once doesn't tell us that you need more; it shows us that lingerie is a bad investment.

4. When Match of the Day comes on, it's a good time for you to pay some bills, call your mother or load the dishwasher.

5. When the waiter asks if everything's OK, a simple 'yes' will suffice.

6. When I'm just turning off onto the slip road, there's no need to shout, "This is our exit."

7. If you want us to take out the rubbish, you have to let us pack the car.

8. Two hot dogs and a beer at a football match does constitute going out to dinner.

9. You probably don't want to know what we're thinking about.

10. It's not in our interests, or yours, to take the Cosmo quiz together.

Questions and Answers...

Q What is the difference between
a battery and a woman?
A A battery always has a positive side.

Q What are the three fastest means of
communication in this technical age?
A The internet, telephone
or tell a woman.

Q What should you give a woman
who has everything?
A A man to show her how to
work it all.

Q What's the difference between a bitch and a whore?
A A whore sleeps with everyone at the party, while a bitch sleeps with everyone at the party except you.

Q What's worse than a Male Chauvinist Pig?
A A woman who won't do what she's told.

Q Why do women close their eyes during sex?
A They don't like to see a man having a good time.

Q What is love?
A The delusion that one woman is different from another.

Questions and Answers...

Q Why do women have orgasms?
A It gives them something else to moan about.

Q Why is a laundromat a bad place to pick up women?
A If they can't afford a washing machine, they'll never be able to support you.

Q How many male chauvinists does it take to change a light bulb?
A None; let her cook in the dark.

Q What's a **man's idea** of helping with **the housework?**

A Lifting **his legs** so **she** can vacuum.

Q What's the **difference between** PMT and BSE?

A One's **mad cow** disease, the other's an **agricultural problem.**

A change of heart…

A husband and wife were having dinner at
a very fine restaurant when this absolutely
stunning young woman came over to their table.
She gave the husband a big kiss, told him
she'd see him later and tottered away.

The wife glared at him:
"Who was that?"

"Oh," replied the husband airily,
"that's my mistress."

"That's it!"
cried the wife, throwing down her napkin.
"I want a divorce."

"I understand your reasons,"
he replied calmly,
"but remember, if you get a divorce, there will
be no more shopping trips to Paris,
no wintering in the Caribbean, no Mercedes
in the garage, no more anything –
the decision is yours."

Just then the wife noticed a mutual friend
entering the restaurant with a gorgeous woman.

"Hang on – who's that with Jim?"
she asked.

"That's his mistress."

"Ours is prettier."

Full circle...

When I was 14, all I wanted was a girl
with a large chest.

When I was 16, I dated a girl with a large
chest, but there was no passion.

So I decided I needed a passionate girl
with a zest for life.

At university, I dated a passionate girl,
but she was too emotional.
Everything was an emergency, she was a
complete drama queen, she cried all the time,
even threatened suicide.

So I decided I needed a girl with some stability.

I found a very stable girl but she was boring. She was totally predictable and never got excited about anything. Life become so dull that I decided I needed a girl with some excitement.

So I found an exciting girl, but I couldn't keep up with her. She rushed from one thing to another, never settled, did mad, impetuous things and flirted with everyone she met. She made me miserable as often as happy. She was great fun initially and very energetic, but directionless.

So I decided to find a girl with some ambition. I found a smart, ambitious girl with her feet planted firmly on the ground. I married her.

But she was so ambitious that she divorced me and took everything I owned.

So now all I want is a girl with a large chest.

Questions and Answers...

Q How do men sort their laundry?
A 'Filthy' and 'Filthy but wearable'.

Q What's the difference between your suit and a woman?
A Women are usually double-breasted.

Q Why does a man on a diet never change a light bulb?
A Because he's always going to start tomorrow.

Q What is it when a man talks nasty to a woman?
A Sexual harrassment

Q What is it when a woman talks nasty to a man?
A £3 a minute.

Q What makes men chase women they have no intention of marrying?
A The same urge that makes dogs chase cars they have no intention of driving.

Questions and Answers…

Q Why is it hard for women to find men who are sensitive, caring and good looking?
A Because those men already have boyfriends.

Q What's a man's idea of a perfect date?
A A woman who answers her door stark naked, holding a hot pizza and a six pack.

Q Why is a woman like a doormat?
A If you lay it in the right place, in the right way, you can wipe your feet on it for the rest of your life.

Reminder for women…

The wife who puts her husband in the dog house will soon find him in the cat house.

Q What's a man's definition of a romantic evening?
A Sex.

Reminder for women…

When women wonder what we're thinking, they discover that the answer is nothing. We're just mooching, daydreaming, brain idling in neutral. And, no, we're not thinking about them.

10 easy ways
to get your own way
(and annoy her
at the same time)...

1. Turn the TV up every time she repeats the question.

2. Ignore her.

3. Walk away.

4. Offer to go to the supermarket and buy only the food you like.

5. Charm her mother and get her on your side.

6. Train the dog to howl when her voice is raised.

7. Say, "Yes, dear!" and do what you like.

8. Check her diary and arrange appointments that clash.

9. Compliment her while she's telling you to do something.

10. Fall asleep.

A good woman's price is above Ruby's.

A story is told that Bernard Shaw once turned to his partner at a dinner table and asked her if she would go to bed with a man for £500.

She smirked and said roguishly, "Well, it would depend on how good looking the man was…"

"Would you do it for ten bob (50p)?" enquired Shaw.

"What do you take me for?" cried the lady indignantly.

"We have already settled that question," said Shaw drily. "All we are discussing now is the price."

An old toast:

Here's to the love that lies in woman's eyes
And lies and lies and lies and lies and lies!

The 11th Commandment:
"Thou shalt not be found out."
18th Century Proverb

"He that would the daughter win
must with the mother first begin."
17th Century Proverb

"A woman's place is in the wrong."
James Thurber

"Swine, women and bees cannot be turned."
17th Century Proverb

30 reasons why it's great being a bloke...

You understand football.

A 5-day holiday requires one overnight bag.

'Phone conversations are done in 30 seconds flat.

You can open all your own jars.

When you're flicking through the channels, you don't have to stop at every one where someone's crying.

You can go to the toilet
without a support group.

You get extra credit for the slightest
act of thoughtfulness.

You never have to clean a toilet.

You can be showered and ready
in 10 minutes flat.

You save time and money by
washing up in bulk every third week.

Wedding plans take care of themselves.

You don't have to shave below your neck.

None of your co-workers
has the power to make you cry.

You can write your name in the snow.

If someone forgets to invite you to something,
it means that they forgot to invite you.
It doesn't mean they hate you, and
they can still be your friend.

What biological clock?

You never have to worry about
other people's feelings.

You get to think about sex
90% of your waking hours.

Flowers fix everything.

Car mechanics tell you the truth.

You don't give a monkey's if someone doesn't notice your new haircut.

You can sit and watch sport on TV with a mate for hours without ever thinking he's cross with you.

One mood, all the time.

Same work, more play.

The remote control is yours and yours alone.

You don't have to remember everyone's birthdays and anniversaries.

You don't need to keep Simply Red, M People or compilations called all 100% woman in the car.

Your mates never say, "Talk to me."

Your mates never say, "What's offside?"

Life will go on if the bed sheets don't get changed once in a while.

Remember:

Only his hairdresser knows for sure....

Bumper sticker:

I lost 250 lbs. in one day –
I divorced her.

Words to live by:

Never argue with a spouse
who is packing your parachute.

"Woman are made to be loved,
not understood."
Oscar Wilde

How to survive women – treat them like your car...

Avoid models that stall during use.

Take care not to allow too much steam or moisture to build up when away from home.

Keep locked in the garage when not in use.

Ensure any problems are clearly expressed on the facia.

Check for pulling attachments.

Ensure that no joy-riders can get their hands on it.

Keep all leather accessories in order.

If necessary, fit a silencer.

For your own safety, never attempt to handle when drunk.

How to survive women – treat them like your car…

Avoid taking it to the pub if you're drinking.

Stay well clear of people carriers.

Be wary of fast models – they will probably have high mileage and excessive amounts of wear.

Never get too attached to ones you have to rent.

Never own a 'wide load' model.

Replace every year with a newer model.

How to survive women – treat her like a woman…

On a transatlantic flight, a 'plane is hit by a severe storm. The turbulence is awful, and things go from bad to worse when one wing is struck by lightning. One woman loses it completely. Screaming she stands up at the front of the plane.

"I'm too young to die!" she wails.

"But, if I'm going to die, I want my last minutes on earth to be memorable! I've had plenty of sex in my life, but no one ever made me feel really like a woman! Well I've had it – is there someone, anyone on this 'plane who can make me feel like a woman?!"

Her speech ends with her voice shrill, breath panting.

For a moment, there is silence except for the terribly thudding of the turbulence, but everyone has forgotten his own peril. They sit staring, riveted, at the desperate woman in the front of the 'plane.

Suddenly a man stands up in the rear of the plane.

"I can make you feel like a woman," he calls to the woman. He's gorgeous; tall, well-muscled, with long flowing black hair and jet black eyes. He starts to walk slowly up the aisle, unbuttoning his shirt one button at a time.

Everyone holds their breath. They watch the man walk by, and then approach the woman who is now breathing heavily in anticipation, licking her lips.

He removes his shirt – muscles rippling across his chest – and as he reaches her, he extends the hand holding the shirt out to the trembling woman.

"Here, iron this."

20 things guys learn from action movies...

Whatever my problem is, it's someone else's fault, so I shall find that person and kill him with my bare hands.

The definition of a beautiful woman is one wearing high heels and an outfit so tight you can see if she's cold or not.

There are two kinds of women – one who wants to go to bed with you, and one who wants to kill you. Both are devastatingly attractive and under 25.

If I argue with the boss in front of my colleagues, he'll respect me – he won't fire me.

If I can find a vital mission to do, it lets me off household duties, showering and calling the next day.

If I go without showering, swear a lot, chew a cigar and treat women badly, they will adore me.

If a women tries to clean my bullet wound and I curse roundly, she will fall in love with me.

Anyone who isn't a cop, mercenary and/or private investigator is a wimp.

If I have a prolonged fist-fight with another guy and neither of us dies, we become best mates.

My arch-enemy will look uncannily like my father, and he will declare his deep respect for me just before I kill him with my bare hands.

When I shoot people, they die quickly and neatly. I am never arrested or troubled by their widow or children. However, if I am shot, it's only a flesh wound that must be tended by a beautiful woman.

If I'm white, I will befriend at least one black guy and vice versa. If I am Latino, the bad guy will kill me half-way through, thus urging the hero to greater levels of revengeful violence.

If an aging scientist is involved, he will have a beautiful daughter who will fall in love with me.

If royalty is involved, there will be a beautiful princess who will fall in love with me.

If I have a kid partner, he will be tightly-muscled, clean-cut and hero-worship me.

If I have to compete against the world champion at any sport/game/skill, I always win. My infuriated opponent will then try to kill me.

If I have to do a surprise attack, it will only be one or two at a time. I am skilled at karate and jujitsu. However, if all else fails, I will discover a firearm hidden somewhere on my body.

If my opponent has a henchman,
he's called Rick or Steve.

Beautiful women will frequently
furrow their brows and ask:
"When did you last sleep/eat?"
rather than when did I
last use the toilet or shower –
although I never seem to do
those things either.

When chasing or fleeing from an
enemy, I can drive any kind of vehicle
with great skill at a reckless 130 mph
without a seat belt.

Warning for men...

One tequila, two tequila,
three tequila, floor.

Two fat blokes are in the pub.
One says to the other:
"Your round."
The other one replies:
"So are you, you fat git."

Reminder:

You don't buy beer – you only rent it.

Definition of intoxication:

You feel sophisticated, but you
can't actually say it.

Female logic exposed...

"My darling,"
asked Jenny,
"What would you do if I died?"

"Well, of course I'd be very upset,"
replied her spouse, not glancing up
from his newspaper.
"Why do you ask?"

"Would you remarry?"

"No, of course not, dear."

"Why wouldn't you remarry?"
persevered Jenny.

"All right, I'd remarry."

"You would?" Jenny is vaguely hurt.

"Yes."

"Would you sleep with her in our bed?"

"I suppose so."

"I see. And would you let her wear my old clothes?"

"I suppose so – if she wanted to."

"Really," said Jenny icily, "and would you take down the pictures of me and replace them with pictures of her?"

"Probably the right thing to do."

Jenny leapt to her feet indignantly. "And I suppose you'd let her play with my golf clubs too!"

"Of course not, dear," replied her husband equably,

"she's left-handed."

Women will never be equal to men
until they can walk down the street
with a bald head and a beer gut
and still think they are beautiful.

You know you're drinking too much
when you get not so much a hang-over
as cerebral fallout.

A woman will be as good as a man
only when she can pee standing up.

Beauty is potent, but money is omnipotent.

Not so much a bachelor pad – more
a home for unmarried socks.

Men wake up as good-looking as they went to bed. Women somehow deteriorate during the night…

Women are like bananas: the older they grow, the less firm they get.

Dieting means getting regular-sized fries with your burger.

Women's make-up should be limited to a certain millimetre depth.

Handbags should be limited to a certain cubic capacity.

Warning for men...

Kids in the back seat cause accidents – accidents in the back seat cause kids.

Women should be limited to one suitcase wherever they went – after all, we don't want them to wear clothes anyway.

Handbags should be registered as offensive weapons.

Woman to man:

"What do you mean, coming home half-drunk?"

"It wasn't my fault; I ran out of money."

In the future, men would ensure that nose and ear hair became an attractive fashion feature.

Never mind...

"Someone stole all my credit cards,
but I won't be reporting it.
The thief spends less than my wife."

We always hold hands.
If I let go, she shops.

She was at the beauty salon for two hours –
and that was just for the estimate.

She got a mudpack and looked
great for two days.
Then the mud fell off.

10 reasons why a bottle of beer is better than a woman...

1. It doesn't talk.

2. It's always refreshing.

3. You can hold it by the neck without a GBH charge.

4. It makes every trip to the pub worthwhile.

5. It's always chilled.

6. You can share one with a mate without World War III starting.

7. It helps relax you after a long day.

8. It's non-judgmental.

9. Even if you get a hang-over, it eventually goes.

10. Once it's gone, it's gone – you're unlucky if it comes back.

Questions and Answers...

Q Why does the bride always wear white?
A Because it's good for the dishwasher to match the cooker and the 'fridge.

Q How can you tell if you're at a bulimic bachelor party?
A The cake jumps out of the girl.

Q How can you tell if a woman's flat-chested?
A When she looks down, the first bumps she sees are her knees.

Q Why did God create women?
A Because sheep can't cook.

Q How does a woman show she's planning for the future?
A Plastic surgery.

Q How many men does it take to open a beer?
A None – it should be open by the time she brings it to you.

Q How can a women tell if she's ugly?
A Men only want to play dress poker with her.

Q Why are girls like rocks?
A The flat ones are better to skip.

Q How do you know if a man has a really ugly wife?
A Her pet name is Spot.

Questions and Answers...

Q How can you tell if a woman's cooking
is really lousy?
A Natives come from the Amazon to
dip their arrows in her sauces.

Q What's the difference between a dog and a fox?
A About five drinks.

Q How can you tell if a woman is too fat?
A Young lovers try to carve
their initials on her legs.

Q How do you turn a fox into an elephant?
A Marry it.

Q How can you tell if a woman is really fat?
A When she goes to Japan, the sumo wrestlers cower in fear.

10 reasons why a burger is better than a woman...

1. It doesn't need to be chatted up before you can enjoy it.

2. It doesn't answer back.

3. You can enjoy one without any frilly bits, but you can add chips if you want.

4. It satisfies an immediate need.

5. It doesn't cost a fortune to spice it up.

6. You can enjoy one anywhere you like without being arrested.

7. You can throw it away if you don't want it all.

8. It's quick and cheap.

9. It doesn't mind if you belch loudly afterwards.

10. After five minutes, you can forget all about it.

10 reasons why coffee is better than a woman...

1. A cup of coffee looks and smells good in the morning.

2. You don't fall asleep after one.

3. Coffee is out of your system by morning.

4. You can turn the coffee maker on and leave the room – when you come back, it's hot.

5. You can **always ditch** **a bad cup** of coffee.

6. If you put **chocolate in** your coffee, it **doesn't put on** weight.

7. Coffee **doesn't mind** if you want **it at** 3 a.m.

8. You **can't get arrested** for ordering **one at** 3 a.m.

9. Your coffee **doesn't get jealous** of a larger **cup.**

10. When **coffee gets old** and **stale,** you can just **throw it away.**

For Men Who Take Life
Too Seriously...

Save the whales.
Collect the whole set.

A day without sunshine is like, night.

On the other hand, you
have different fingers.

I just got lost in thought.
It was unfamiliar territory.

42.7 percent of all statistics
are made up on the spot.

99 percent of lawyers give
the rest a bad name.

I feel like I'm diagonally parked
in a parallel universe.

You have the right to remain silent.
Anything you say will be misquoted,
then used against you.

I wonder how much deeper the ocean
would be without sponges.

Honk if you love peace and quiet.

A conclusion is simply the place where
you got tired of thinking.

For Men Who Take Life
Too Seriously...

Despite the cost of living, have you noticed how popular it remains?

Nothing is foolproof to a talented fool.

Atheism is a non-prophet organisation.

I intend to live forever – so far, so good.

He who laughs last thinks slowest.

Eagles may soar, but weasels don't get sucked into jet engines.

I drive 'way too fast
to worry about cholesterol.

Depression is merely anger
without enthusiasm.

Borrow money from a pessimist –
he won't expect it back.

My mind is like a steel trap –
rusty and illegal across the UK.

Did you hear about the dyslexic pimp
who bought a warehouse?

The early bird may get the worm,
but the second mouse gets the cheese.

Quantum mechanics:
The dreams stuff is made of...

The only substitute for good manners is fast reflexes.

Support bacteria – they're the only culture some people have.

When everything's coming your way, realise you're in the wrong lane and going the wrong way.

If at first you don't succeed, destroy all evidence that you tried.

Experience is something you don't get until just after you need it.

For every action there is an equal and opposite criticism.

War doesn't decide who's right. War decides who's left.

The man who drives like hell is bound to get there.

If the meek shall inherit the earth, the (Arsenal) strikers will be land barons.

If men were really in charge, women drivers would be limited to getting your dinner from the supermarket, picking your kids up from school and collecting us from the pub.

Bills travel through the mail at twice the speed of cheques.

He who hesitates is probably right.

Questions and Answers...

Q How do you know when a woman's going to say something intelligent?
A She starts her sentence with: "A man once told me..."

Q What's the difference between the team clown and the team nerd?
A The team clown tells jokes that everyone gets.
The team nerd tells jokes only he gets.

Q How do you confuse a blonde?
A You don't, they're born that way.

Warning for male drivers…

There are only two kinds of pedestrians – the quick and the dead.

Man to man:
"Where's the King's Arms?"
"Usually around the Queen."

Postcard in public phone box:
Like a nice time, dearie?
'Phone 123.

Q What's the main difference between men and boys?
A Men's toys cost more.

Questions and Answers...

Q Who do men put women on pedestals?
A So they can look up their skirts.

Q What's the definition of a lazy man?
A One who gets someone to read the DIY manual to him.

Q What's the difference between Big Foot and an intelligent woman?
A Big Foot has been spotted a couple of times.

Definition of an intellectual…

A man who can listen to the William Tell Overture without thinking of the Lone Ranger.

"Some people think football is a matter of life and death. I don't like that attitude. I can assure them it is much more serious than that."

Attributed to Bill Shankley 1973

Definition of a happy motorist:

A man with flies in his teeth.

10 politically correct terms for women...

She isn't hairy,
she's follicly gifted.

She doesn't get PMT,
she becomes hormonally homicidal.

She doesn't have a killer body,
she is terminally attractive.

She's not a bad cook,
she is microwave compatible.

She isn't a bad driver,
she is automotively challenged.

She isn't a perfect 10,
she is numerically superior.

She doesn't wear too much make-up,
she is cosmetically over-saturated.

She doesn't ever gain weight,
she becomes a metabolic underachiever.

She doesn't shave her legs,
she experiences
temporary stubble reduction.

She doesn't have a toned body,
she is anatomically inflexible.

Men vs Women

How to satisfy a woman:

caress, praise, pamper, relish, savour, massage, make plans, empathise, serenade, compliment, support, feed, tantalise, bath, humour, placate, stimulate, stroke, console, purr, hug, coddle, excite, pacify, 'phone, listen, anticipate, nuzzle, smooch, toast, minister to, forgive, miss football for, leave, beseech, entertain, charm, crawl, oblige, fascinate, grovel, coax, clothe, butter-up, understand, take dancing, beg, plead, borrow, steal, climb, repair, etc. etc.

How to satisfy a man:

take your clothes off.

Remember...

"Women who can, do.
Those who cannot become feminists."
Anon.

"You will find that the woman
who is really kind to dogs is always one
who has failed to inspire me."
Max Beerbohm

"A woman is only a woman,
but a good cigar is a smoke."
Rudyard Kipling

"A man without a woman is like a neck
without a pain."
Anon.

Remember...

"A very little wit is valued in a woman;
as we are pleased with a few words spoken
plain by a parrot."

Jonathan Swift

"How like the groans of love are those
of the dying."

Malcolm Lowry, Under the Volcano

"Women have a passion for mathematics.
They divide their age in half, double the price of
their clothes, and always add at least five
years to the age of their best friend."

Marcel Achard

"To embrace a woman is to embrace a sack of manure."

Odo of Cluny

10 Reasons why women are like football pitches...

There is a **vast difference** in ground with regards to **lengths and widths**, although they conform to the **same basic** requirements.

Take care not **to be red-carded** in the tackle.

Be careful as, **after a few pints**, a ground may appear to be of **Premiership** standard which in reality **would not** be eligible for the **West End Premier League.**

Only a very **few grounds** offer **five-a-side** facilities.

Singing songs about other players
is banned.

Extra time may occur even if the
scores are not drawn.

Do not mention other grounds you have
played on, or are currently playing on.

Spectators are not usually present.

Visiting a ground too often may
result in the purchase of
a season ticket.

Some protection should be worn.

Hazardous Materials Information Bulletin.

Material Safety Data Sheet

Woman – A Chemical Analysis

Issued for the Protection of Men

Element: Woman
Chemical Symbol: Wo
Discoverer: Adam
Research Centre: University of Life
Atomic Mass: Accepted as 53.6 kg
                      *(Note: may vary from
                      40 kg to 200 kg)*
Occurrence: Widespread, with particular
                      density in urban areas

1. Physical Properties

1.1 Surface usually covered with brightly-coloured painted film.

1.2 Boils at nothing; also freezes without known reasons.

1.3 Melts if special treatment applied, especially when combined with sugars.

1.4 Bitter if used incorrectly.

1.5 Found in various states ranging from virgin metal to common ore.

1.6 Properties may become camouflaged as age of sample increases.

2. Chemical Properties

2.1 Has great affinity for gold, silver and all precious stones.

2.2 Effortlessly absorbs huge quantities of expensive substances.

2.3 Can explode spontaneously without prior warning and for no known reason.

2.4 Insoluble in liquid, but malleability greatly increased by saturation in alcohol.

2.5 Most powerful money-reducing agent known to man.

2.6 Can be returned to inert state by introduction of chocolate

3. Common Uses

3.1 Highly ornamental, especially in sports cars
and on social occasions.

3.2 Can be used as an aid to relaxation,
and can even induce sleep.

3.3 Very effective cleaning agent.

3.4 Useful catalyst in food production.

3.5 Can be trained to reproduce itself.

2. Test/Analysis Results

4.1 Pure specimen turns rosy pink when
discovered in natural state.

4.2 Can turn green when placed alongside
a better specimen.

4.3 Can turn white if careful treatment
is withdrawn suddenly.

4.5 Produces brine in large
quantities if agitated.

5. Potential Hazards

5.1 Highly dangerous except in well-trained and experienced hands.

5.2 It is illegal to possess more than one sample – although several can be maintained in different locations, provided they do not come into contact with each other.

5.3 Can be detrimental to health and shorten lifespan

5.4 Constant attention minimises combustibility.

10 reasons why owning a dog is better than a woman...

If it goes off, it comes back only when you call it.

It doesn't care if you forget it for five minutes.

It doesn't need to call its mother.

It doesn't need cosmetics or jewellery.

It is completely happy eating food out of a tin.

It's always pleased to see you – the later you are, the better.

It's happy if you just take it out for a walk.

You don't have to buy it dinner.

You can teach it tricks that impress your mates.

It's happy to sit under the table in the pub and keep its biscuit shoot shut.

10 reasons why football
is better than marriage...

1. You can talk to your mates about football and they always understand.

2. You never run out of things to talk about.

3. You can spend endless happy hours replaying matches, reliving moments.

4. The opposition gets sent off if they foul you.

5. Your loyalty to your club lasts a lifetime.

6. You can get rid of your tensions without a GBH charge.

7. You can sing, swear and belch as loudly as you like – without fear.

8. You understand offside.

9. There's always a referee and a rule book to sort out disputes.

10. You can choose to change clubs with the only expense being your supporter's shirt.

The male stages of life...

Age	Seduction line
18	My parents are away
25	My girlfriend is away
35	My fiancèe is away
48	My wife is away
66	My second wife has just died

Age	Favourite sport
18	Sex
25	Sex
35	Sex
48	Sex
66	Sex

Age	Favourite drink
18	Beer
25	Beer
35	Whisky
48	Double whisky
66	Milk of Magnesia

Age	Definition of a successful date
18	Tongue
25	Breakfast
35	She hasn't set back my therapy
48	I didn't have to meet her kids
66	I got home alive

Age	The ideal age for getting married
18	25
25	35
35	48
48	66
66	18

Age	Ideal date
18	Stephen King triple bill at the cinema
25	Let's split the bill and go back to my place
35	Just come over
45	Just come over and cook
66	Sex in the company jet on the way to the Bahamas

20 good reasons why you can't go out with her...

I've been scheduled for a karma transplant.

It's my parakeet's bowling night.

I'm trying to see how long I can go without saying yes.

I have a subsequent engagement.

My plot to take over the world is thickening.

My subconscious says no.

I left my body in my other clothes.

I've just picked up a book called Glue in Many Lands, and I can't put it down.

I promised to help my mate
fold his road maps.

I'm trying to be less popular.

I'm observing National Apathy Week.

I've got to count the bristles
on my toothbrush.

Having fun gives me Prickly Heat.

My palm reader advised me to stay home.

I prefer to remain an enigma.

I'm trying to cut down on
the number of women I see.

My doctor's warned me against
getting excited.

I'm too old/young for that sort of thing.

Remind me who you are again?

My beer appreciation class meets tonight.

20 facts about women
that men should know...

Women love to shop, and they especially love a bargain – they feel in control and they usually have no need for the item in question.

Women never have anything to wear – query the racks of clothes hanging in the wardrobe and you 'just don't understand'.

Women need to cry – but they won't do it alone unless they know you can hear them.

Women love to talk – silence intimidates them and they feel a need to fill it, even if they've nothing to say.

Women don't need sex as often as men.
Just knowing the man wants to have sex fulfils
their emotional needs.

Women can't keep secrets – they eat away at
them from inside. But if they tell only two or
three people, it's not being untrustworthy.

Women never understand why men like toys.
Men understand that they wouldn't need toys
if women had an on/off button.

Women don't really care about a sense
of humour in a guy, despite what they say.
You don't see women trampling over
Pierce Brosnan to get
to Jasper Carrott.

If a man goes on a 7-day trip, he packs 5 days' worth of clothes and wears some things twice. A woman takes 21 outfits because she doesn't know what she'll feel like wearing each day.

Women love cats. Men say they love cats but secretly give them a kick when she's not looking.

Women do not want an honest answer to the question: "How do I look?"

Women cannot read maps, they will always get you lost, and you will always have an argument about it.

"Oh, nothing," has 100 more meanings in women-language than any other.

All women are overweight by definition; don't agree with them about it.

If it's not Valentine's Day and you see a man buying flowers, you can probably start up a conversation by asking, "What did you do?"

Origin of the word woman: woo-man.

Women can get out of speeding tickets by pouting. This will get men arrested.

Women fake orgasm because men fake foreplay.

It's OK for women to dance together and not be gay. You don't see straight men dancing together.

The most embarrassing thing for a woman is to find another wearing the same dress at a formal party. You never hear men say: "Oh, my God, there's another man wearing a black dinner jacket, how awful!"

On medical advice...

A man was warned by his doctor against too much high living.

"Can I guarantee,"

he asked the doctor,

"that if I give up drinking, smoking and sex, I shall live longer?"

"No,"

replied the doctor,

"but it will seem longer."

10 reasons why dogs and women are alike...

They look stupid in hats.

They can eat 5 pounds of chocolate at a sitting.

They tend to have 'hip problems'.

They don't understand football.

They look good in a fur coat.

They are good at pretending to listen
to your every word.

They don't believe silence is golden.

You can never tell what they are thinking.

They put too much value on kissing.

They can't balance their cheque-book.

20 ways to know
if you're getting old...

Your potted plants stay alive.

Your friends marry and divorce instead
of getting together and breaking up.

6 a.m. is when you get up,
not when you go to bed.

You hear your favourite song
in the lift at work.

You're the one calling the police about
the kids with the noisy stereo.

Having sex in a single bed is absurd.

You keep more food than beer in your 'fridge.

You watch the weather forecast.

You don't know what time
the kebab shop closes any more.

Your car insurance goes down
and your car payments go up.

You feed your dog proper dog food
instead of McDonald's.

Dinner and a film constitutes the whole
date instead of just the beginning.

You go to a chemist for aspirin and antacids,
instead of condoms and pregnancy kits.

A £2.50 bottle of wine is no longer
'pretty good stuff.'

You actually eat breakfast foods at breakfast time.

Grocery lists are longer than beer, beans, instant soup and bread.

"I just can't drink the way I used to," replaces: "I'll never drink that much again."

Over 90% of the time you spend at a computer is for real work.

You don't get drunk at home first to save money before going to a bar.

You go from 130 days' holiday to 20.

I'll have what he's having...

Getting married is very much
like going to a restaurant with friends.
You order what you want; then,
when you see what the other fellow has,
you wish you had ordered that.